Arminianism
or
Calvinism?

An Introduction to
Arminianism and Calvinism

Sylvia Penny

ISBN: 978-1-78364-214-4

www.obt.org.uk

****

THE OPEN BIBLE TRUST
Fordland Mount, Upper Basildon,
Reading, RG8 8LU, UK.

Arminianism or Calvinism?

Contents

Page

Introduction

What are Calvinism and Arminianism? What are the differences? And why does it matter? Basically they are two different theological views regarding God's role and our own in the whole process of salvation. Both are based on the Bible, but the differences arise due to their interpretation of what the Bible says.

Calvinism was popularised by John Calvin (1509-1564) who was a French Reformer, and followed after Martin Luther (1483-1546) who initiated the Reformation. Arminianism is named after Jacob Arminius (1560-1609) who was a Dutch theologian.

Calvinism

Calvinism has a very high view of the sovereignty of God, and covers a whole range of thought on every aspect of life. Five of its main points, known by the acronym TULIP, are displayed on the next page:

1. T otal depravity	Sin against God has corrupted humans so much that we have an inability to choose God unless he chooses us.
2. U nconditional election	Election for salvation is not based on any merit in us or on God foreknowing we would believe in Christ.
3. L imited atonement	Christ only died for those elected for salvation.
4. I rresistable grace	We cannot resist God's call if we are part of His elect.
5. P erseverance of the Saints	We cannot lose our salvation. If we are elected, we are secure for eternity.

Calvinism says that, as a result of the fall, man's will is in total bondage to his evil nature, and therefore it is impossible for man, of his own volition, to believe in God and follow Him. Therefore God must choose certain people to follow Him, and then predestine them to faith. Faith is not something man has in and of himself, but is a part of God's gift of salvation – faith is God's gift to the sinner, not the sinner's gift to God. Once chosen by God, man cannot lose his salvation. He is secure for eternity.

Arminianism

On the other hand, Jacob Arminius provided a system of Biblical interpretation that came to very different conclusions. His was a reaction to some of what are perceived as the harsher aspects of Calvinism. Contrary to Calvin he asserted that God's sovereignty and man's free will are compatible, and that human dignity demands free will.

Later John Wesley, and Methodism, were strongly influenced by Arminianism, and later still, the Salvation Army.

In 1610 a theological statement, the Remonstrance, was drawn up and stated five principles:

1. Partial depravity	Humans are deeply tainted by sin, but not so much that we are unable to choose, of our own free will, whether to accept Christ as our Saviour or not.
2. Conditional election	Election for salvation is conditional upon God foreseeing that we would respond to His call. God foresees our faith - He does not give it to us.
3. Unlimited atonement	Christ died for the whole world, but only gives salvation to those that believe in Him.
4. Grace can be resisted	People have free will, and can resist the Holy Spirit's call to salvation.
5. Conditional salvation	Christians can lose their salvation if they fall away from God or return to persistent habitual sin.

Therefore Arminianism says that, although human nature was seriously affected by the fall, man still has free will, and through the grace of God is able to repent and believe if he so chooses. God does not interfere with man's freedom to choose good over evil.

Man can co-operate with God's Spirit and be regenerated and have eternal life, or he can resist God's grace and perish. Faith is an act of man, and is exercised before salvation. As a result of man's faith, God ultimately gives him righteousness in eternal life. However, if man does not continue in his faith, but falls away and returns to persistent habitual sin, then he can lose his salvation as a result.

Which of these views is correct?

Both these views of salvation, and the parts that God and man play, are firmly based on the Scriptures. It is the interpretation of the Scriptures that differs, so how do we determine which is the correct view? Or do both views have points for and against them? We can form our opinion by looking at the Scriptures quoted on each side of the argument.

Below, for each of the five points listed above, the Calvinistic view is stated first, together with some of the Scriptures used to support this view. Then the alternative Arminian view is stated, again with some of the Scriptures used to support it, and a comparison with Calvinism.

(1a) Total depravity (Calvinism)

Man has an evil nature and therefore cannot seek God

Calvinism argues that man is so intrinsically evil that he is simply unable to seek God. He is totally dependent upon God electing him for eternal life. Some of the verses this view is based upon are quoted below.

Man's evil nature

> Mark 7:21,22 - For from within, out of men's hearts, come evil thoughts, sexual immorality, theft, murder, adultery, greed, malice, deceit, lewdness, envy, slander, arrogance and folly.

> Jeremiah 17:9 - The heart is deceitful above all things and beyond cure. Who can understand it?

Romans 6:20 - When you were slaves to sin, you were free from the control of righteousness.

Man cannot seek God

Psalm 14:2,3 - The Lord looks down from heaven on the sons of men to see if there are any who understand, any who seek God. *All have turned aside, they have together become corrupt; there is no-one who does good, not even one.*

1 Corinthians 2:14 - *The man without the Spirit does not accept the things that come from the Spirit of God*, for they are foolishness to him, and he cannot understand them, because they are spiritually discerned.

Ephesians 2:3-5 - All of us also lived among them (unbelievers) at one time, gratifying the cravings of our sinful nature and following its desires and thoughts. Like the rest, we were by nature objects of wrath. But because of his great love for us, *God, who is rich in mercy, made us alive with Christ even when we were dead in transgressions* – it is by grace you have been saved.

(1b) Partial depravity (Arminianism)

Man has an evil nature, but he is still able to seek to follow God of his own free will

Arminians agree that man has an evil nature, based upon the same verses as those quoted above. However, they argue that although some men do not choose to follow God, there are others that do. Man can choose to believe in Christ as his Saviour if he so wishes. This is termed "partial depravity", meaning that man is not so sinful that he is totally unable to choose to follow God if he wishes. This view is based upon verses such as those quoted below.

Deuteronomy 30:19,20 - This day I call heaven and earth as witnesses against you that I have set before you life and death, blessings and curses. *Now choose life*, so that you and your children may live and that you may love the Lord your God, listen to his voice, and hold fast to him.

Joshua 24:15 - But if serving the Lord seems undesirable to you, *then choose for yourselves* this day whom you will serve, whether the gods your forefathers served beyond the River, or the gods of the Amorites, in whose land you are living. But as for me and my household, we will serve the Lord.

Proverbs 8:10 - *Choose my instruction* instead of silver, knowledge rather than choice gold.

John 7:17 - *If anyone chooses* to do God's will, he will find out whether my teaching comes from God or whether I speak on my own.

Many verses refer to the evil of man, and how, without God, there is no good in him. It is very clear that without God, man is "a slave to sin". However, some verses in Scripture refer to the role God plays in reaching out to man and offering him the way of salvation, and other verses refer to the role man plays in responding to the offer made by God. It is a two way process of God's offer and man's acceptance; of God's forgiveness and man's repentance; of God's love and man's obedience. It appears that despite man's sinfulness, he does have a choice. He has been given free will by God, and can choose to do God's will if he so wishes.

(2a) Unconditional election (Calvinism)

God elects people for salvation and faith is part of the gift of salvation

Calvinism says that God elects those to be saved, and that this does not depend upon anything that the individual believes or does. It is purely in accordance with His will. Faith itself is a gift of God, and not something that comes from man. Some of the verses that this view is based upon are quoted below.

Election by God

> Ephesians 1:4,5 - For he chose us in him before the creation of the world to be holy and blameless in his sight. In love he predestined us to be adopted as his sons through Jesus Christ, in accordance with his pleasure and will

Romans 8:29,30 - For those God foreknew he also predestined to be conformed to the likeness of his Son, that he might be the firstborn among many brothers. And those he predestined, he also called; those he called, he also justified; those he justified, he also glorified.

Faith is a gift of God

Ephesians 2:8 - For it is by grace you have been saved, through faith – and this not from yourselves, it is the gift of God

Philippians 1:29 - For it has been granted to you on behalf of Christ not only to believe on him, but also to suffer for him

John 6:28-29 - Then they asked him, "What must we do to do the works God requires?" Jesus answered, "The work of God is this: to believe in the one he has sent."

(2b) Conditional election (Arminianism)

Election is based on God's foreknowledge of man's faith in Him

Arminianism says that God selected only those whom He knew would of themselves freely believe the gospel. Election is therefore conditional upon what man does. It is those that God *foreknew* would believe that He predestined to be conformed to the likeness of his Son.

Election by God

This view is also based upon the same Scriptures quoted above, but with a different interpretation of what they mean. The difference lies in understanding the *reason* that God chose (or elected) people "to be holy and blameless" and "to be conformed to the likeness of his Son". Arminians will point to the foreknowledge mentioned in Romans 8:29, and understand that this refers to God's foreknowledge of a person's acceptance of the gospel of salvation, and their belief in Christ as their Saviour.

Ephesians 1:13 says "And you also were included in Christ *when you heard the word of truth, the gospel of your salvation.* Having believed, you were marked in him with a seal …". God, knowing in advance who would believe in Him of their own free will, then predestined all these "to be adopted as his sons through Jesus Christ". Their election is therefore conditional upon their belief and faith in Him.

Faith is *not* a gift of God

Similarly, the view that faith in God is something that man possesses, and *not* a gift from God is based on the same verses quoted above, but with a different interpretation of them.

> Ephesians 2:8 - For it is by grace you have been saved, through faith – and this not from yourselves, it is the gift of God

Here, Arminians say that the gift of God is salvation, not faith. Salvation is achieved by the grace of God through the faith of the believer. In this verse, in the Greek, the word "this" is neuter, and as such it refers to "salvation", rather than "faith," which is feminine.

There are in fact no verses in Scripture that describe faith as being a gift from God. It is always described as belonging to the believer. Hebrews 11 is the great chapter on faith, and in verse 1 says, "Now faith is being sure of what we hope for and certain of what we do not see."

The chapter then goes on to give many examples of people with such faith. Nowhere does it describe this faith as being a gift from God.

> Philippians 1:29 - For it has been granted to you on behalf of Christ not only to believe on him, but also to suffer for him

Arminians say this does not mean that God grants that some men will believe in Him, and that others will not, but rather that He grants all those that *do* believe in Him the privilege of suffering for Him.

> John 6:28-29 - Then they asked him, "What must we do to do the works God requires?" Jesus answered, "The work of God is this: to believe in the one he has sent."

Here the Arminian view is that "the work of God" refers to the work God requires from man (in this case it is belief), and not work that God does on behalf of man.

(3a) Limited Atonement (Calvinism)

Jesus died only for those elected for salvation

Calvinists believe that Christ's redeeming work was intended to save the elect only and actually secured salvation for them. His death paid the penalty of sin in the place of certain specified sinners. Some of the verses this view is based upon are quoted below.

> Matthew 1:21 - She will give birth to a son, and you are to give him the name Jesus, because *he will save his people from their sins.*

> Matthew 26:28 - This is my blood of the covenant, which is poured out *for many* for the forgiveness of sins.

John 17:9 - I am not praying for the world, *but for those you have given me*, for they are yours.

Acts 20:28 - Be shepherds *of the church of God*, which he bought with his own blood.

Isaiah 53:12 - For he bore the sin *of many*.

Calvinists say that these verses show that Christ died for "his people", for "many", for "those given", and for "the church of God", and that these only include those previously elected by God for salvation. They do not include the whole world.

(3b) Unlimited Atonement (Arminianism)

Jesus died for the whole world, but only gives salvation to those that believe in Him

Arminians say that Christ's redeeming work made it *possible* for everyone to be saved, but although this is true and Christ died for *all men*, only those who believe on Him are credited with righteousness and are saved. His death enabled God to pardon sinners and credit them with righteousness *on the condition they believe.*

Romans 4:23,24 says, "The words 'it was credited to him' were written not for him alone, but also for us, to whom God will credit righteousness – *for us who believe in him* who raised Jesus our Lord from the dead." This truth of the Lord crediting righteousness in return for belief runs throughout Scripture. Genesis 15:6

says, "Abram believed the Lord, and he credited it to him as righteousness." Thus redemption only becomes effective if man chooses to accept it. The verses quoted in section (3a) above are interpreted by Arminians in the light of this, and are taken to refer to those who accept and believe that Christ died for their sins.

However, there are many other verses that specifically say that Christ's death was for the whole world, some of which are quoted below. Some of these also refer to those who accept this and believe it, and others who do not.

> John 1:29 – The next day John saw Jesus coming towards him and said, "Look, the Lamb of God, *who takes away the sin of the world*!"

> John 3:16-17 – For *God so loved the world* that he gave his one and only Son, that *whoever believes in him shall not perish but have eternal life.* For God did not send his Son into the world to condemn the world, *but to save the world through him.*

John 8:12 – When Jesus spoke again to the people, he said, "*I am the light of the world. Whoever follows me will never walk in darkness*, but will have the light of life."

1 Timothy 2:5,6 - For there is one God and one mediator between God and men, the man Christ Jesus, who gave himself as a ransom *for all men.*

1 John 2:2 - He (Christ) is the atoning sacrifice for our sins, *and not only for ours but also for the sins of the whole world.*

(4a) Irresistible Grace (Calvinism)

People cannot resist God's call if they are part of the elect

Calvinists say that in addition to the outward general call to salvation which is made to everyone who hears the gospel, the Holy Spirit makes a special inward call to the elect that inevitably brings them to salvation. This inward call cannot be rejected – it always results in conversion. The Holy Spirit graciously causes the elect sinner to cooperate, to believe, to repent, and to come freely and willingly to Christ. God's grace is therefore irresistible, and never fails to result in the salvation of those to whom it is extended. Some of the verses on which this view is based are quoted below.

> John 1:12-13 - Yet to all who received him, to those who believed in his name, he gave the right to become children of God – *children born not of natural descent, nor of*

human decision or a husband's will, *but born of God.*

Romans 9:14-16 - What then shall we say? Is God unjust? Not at all! For he says to Moses, "I will have mercy on whom I have mercy, and I will have compassion on whom I have compassion." *It does not, therefore, depend on man's desire or effort, but on God's mercy.*

Phil 2:12-13 - Continue to work out your salvation with fear and trembling, *for it is God who works in you to will and to act according to his good purpose.*

Acts 13:48 - When the Gentiles heard this, they were glad and honoured the word of the Lord; *and all who were appointed for eternal life believed.*

However, each of these verses is understood differently by Arminians. The verses in John 1 do not say that people become children of God through God's will alone, but rather that first they have to believe in his name.

The verses in Romans are taken from Exodus 33:19 by Paul, and do not refer to salvation. They refer to specific people being chosen by God for specific purposes.

Similarly the verses in Philippians do not refer to salvation, but refer to continuing to work out our salvation after initial conversion, and God continues to work in us to enable us to do this.

Lastly, the verse in Acts 13 depends upon the meaning of the word *appointed,* which here has the sense of "enrolment". F. F. Bruce in *The Book of Acts* says on this verse:

> 'There is papyrus evidence for this verb in the sense of "inscribe" or "enrol". ... The idea of being enrolled in the book of life or the like is found in several Biblical passages.'

Therefore, what is being said in this verse is that all those who were written in the book of life believed. As said previously, God foreknew those who would believe (see section 2 on conditional election) and based on this foreknowledge, their names were written in the book of life.

(4b) Grace can be resisted (Arminianism)

People have free will and can resist the Holy Spirit's call to salvation

Arminianism says that the Holy Spirit does all He can to bring every sinner to salvation. But as man has free will he can successfully resist the Spirit's call. The Spirit cannot regenerate the sinner until he believes. Man's free will therefore limits the Spirit in the application of Christ's saving work. God's grace is therefore not irresistible. It can and often is resisted and thwarted by man.

There are many verses that refer to man exercising his own free will, either to reject God's purpose, or to accept it. It is not forced upon them. A few examples are given below.

Man's free will

Luke 7:30 - But the Pharisees and experts in the law *rejected God's purpose for themselves*, because they had not been baptised by John.

1 Timothy 2:3,4 - This is good, and pleases God our Saviour, *who wants all men to be saved* and to come to a knowledge of the truth. (Although God wants this, it does not happen, because of man's free will.)

Joshua 24:15,22 - But if serving the Lord seems undesirable to you, *then choose for yourselves* this day whom you will serve … But as for me and my household, we will serve the Lord … Then Joshua said, "You are witnesses against yourselves that *you have chosen to serve the Lord.*"

Luke 10:42 - *Mary has chosen what is better*, and it will not be taken away from her.

There are a couple of verses in 1 Chronicles 28 where David gives Solomon some advice about the Lord, and they combine both the idea of man seeking God, and God choosing man.

> 1Chronicles 28:9,10 - "And you, my son Solomon, acknowledge the God of your father, and serve him with wholehearted devotion and with a willing mind, for the Lord searches every heart and understands every motive behind the thoughts. If you seek him, he will be found by you; but if you forsake him, he will reject you for ever. Consider now, for the Lord has chosen you to build a temple as a sanctuary. Be strong and do the work."

Although these verses refer specifically to Solomon, they can also be applied to people in general. God knows every person's thoughts, what motivates people, and what makes them behave the way they do. It is also clear that if man seeks for God, He will be found.

However, in Solomon's case, he was also specifically chosen for a particular task – to build a temple for the Lord. We have to recognise that, in some circumstances, God chose particular individuals to perform specific tasks for Him in His service, but that this cannot be applied to people in general.

So it is that people have free will to accept or reject the Holy Spirit's call to salvation. He does not force His power upon people. In Acts 7:51 Stephen, when speaking to the Sanhedrin, says "You always *resist* the Holy Spirit", and in 1 Thessalonians 5:19 Paul pleads that they "Do not put out the Spirit's fire" showing that He can be resisted if people wish to do so.

(5a) Perseverance of the Saints (Calvinism)

You cannot lose your salvation

Calvinism says that once a person is saved they cannot lose their salvation. It is secure. The verses in Ephesians 1:13,14 quoted below make it clear that once a person has believed in Christ as their Saviour they are marked by the seal of the Holy Spirit, Who then guarantees their inheritance. If this is guaranteed by the Holy Spirit, then it must be safe and secure. Romans 4:16 also refers to this guarantee. It says:

> Therefore, the promise comes by faith, so that it may be by grace and may be *guaranteed* to all Abraham's offspring – not only to those who are of the law but also to those who are of the faith of Abraham. He is the father of us all.

Romans 8:38,39 confirms this security by saying:

For I am convinced that neither death nor life, neither angels nor demons, neither the present nor the future, nor any powers, neither height nor depth, nor anything else in all creation, will be able to separate us from the love of God that is in Christ Jesus our Lord." If *nothing* can separate us from the love of God, then it must be safe and secure. Some of the verses on which the security of salvation is based are quoted below.

John 6:39,40 – And this is the will of him who sent me, that I shall lose none of all that he has given me, but raise them up at the last day. For my Father's will is that everyone who looks to the Son and believes in him shall have eternal life, and I will raise him up at the last day.

John 6:47 – I tell you the truth, he who believes has everlasting life.

John 10:27,28 - My sheep listen to my voice; I know them, and they follow me. I give them eternal life, and they shall never perish; no-one can snatch them out of my hand.

Romans 8:1 – Therefore, there is now no condemnation for those who are in Christ Jesus.

1 Corinthians 10:13 – No temptation has seized you except what is common to man. And God is faithful; he will not let you be tempted beyond what you can bear. But when you are tempted, he will also provide a way out so that you can stand up under it.

Ephesians 1:13,14 – And you also were included in Christ when you heard the word of truth, the gospel of your salvation. Having believed, you were marked in him with a seal, the promised Holy Spirit, who is a deposit guaranteeing our inheritance until the redemption of those who are God's possession – to the praise of his glory.

(5b) Conditional Salvation (Arminianism)

Loss of salvation

Arminianism says that those who believe and are truly saved can lose their salvation by failing to keep up their faith, or returning to persistent habitual sin.

This view is based upon many verses that refer to loss, and burning up, being thrown away, falling away, shrinking back and being destroyed. We cannot look at all of these here, but one is given below from John's gospel.

> John 15:1-6 – I am the true vine, and my Father is the gardener. He cuts off every branch in me that bears no fruit, while every branch that does bear fruit he prunes so that it will be even more fruitful. You are already clean because of the word I have

spoken to you. Remain in me, and I will remain in you. No branch can bear fruit by itself; it must remain in the vine. Neither can you bear fruit unless you remain in me. I am the vine; you are the branches. If a man remains in me and I in him, he will bear much fruit; apart from me you can do nothing. If anyone does not remain in me, he is like a branch that is thrown away and withers; such branches are picked up, thrown into the fire and burned.

Loss of reward in eternal life

There are also many similar passages in Hebrews, which exhort believers to go on to maturity in their faith, and not to remain an infant "who lives on milk" (Hebrews 5:13). These are, without exception, referring to loss of reward in eternal life, not loss of eternal life itself.

Perhaps the two passages which suggest most strongly that it is possible to lose one's salvation are Hebrews 6:4-6 and 10:26-31. However, these need to be set beside Hebrews 10:14 which states, "by one sacrifice he has made perfect for ever those who are being made holy." It would seem that those being addressed in Hebrews chapters 6 and 10 were still undecided. These people understood enough to be culpable. They were in grave danger of reverting to Judaism and in so doing rejecting belief in Christ altogether.

There are a number of passages which are very clear on distinguishing between the gift of eternal life (which cannot be taken away), and the rewards to be received in eternal life (which can be lost). Two of them are 2 Timothy 2:11-13 and 1 Corinthians 3:11-15.

> 2 Timothy 2:11-13 - Here is a trustworthy saying: If we died with him, we will also live with him; if we endure, we will also reign with him. If we disown him, he will also disown us; if we are faithless, he will remain faithful, for he cannot disown himself.

In this passage, "If we disown him, he will also disown us" refers to God disowning us.

However, it follows on from "If we endure, we will also reign with him". It is saying if we are faithful in our Christian life we will receive a reward (reign), but if we are not faithful and don't endure, then we effectively choose to forfeit our reward and are "disowned" of it. However, it is very clear that even if we are faithless, he will remain faithful.

> 1 Corinthians 3:11-15 – For no-one can lay any foundation other than the one already laid, which is Jesus Christ. If any man builds on this foundation using gold, silver, costly stones, wood, hay or straw, his work will be shown for what it is, because the Day will bring it to light. It will be revealed with fire, and the fire will test the quality of each man's work. If what he has built survives, he will receive his reward. If it is burned up, he will suffer loss; he himself will be saved, but only as one escaping through the flames.

This passage is very similar to the one in 2 Timothy. Any shoddy workmanship is burned up. Any good works survive, and will receive their reward. However, even if it is all burned up, although a person will suffer loss of reward, he himself will be saved.

Concluding comparison of the two views

Calvinism states that....

Salvation is accomplished by the almighty power of God the Father, God the Son and God the Holy Spirit. The Father chooses certain people, the Son died for them, and the Holy Spirit makes Christ's death effective by bringing the elect to faith and repentance, so causing them to obey the gospel willingly. Election, redemption and regeneration are the work of God and are all by grace. So it is entirely God, not man, who determines who will receive the gift of eternal life. Salvation is therefore safe and secure, and once received as a gift from God, it cannot be lost.

Arminianism states that .....

Salvation is accomplished through a combination of God (who makes the first step) and man (who must respond). It is man's response that determines whether he is saved or not. God has provided the possibility of salvation for everyone, but it only becomes effective when man, of his own free will, chooses to accept the gift of God, and His offer of grace. It is man's will that plays a decisive role, and so it is man himself who determines whether or not he will receive the gift of eternal life. However, it is therefore possible for a person to lose their salvation if they do not continue in a state of belief, and decide to turn away from God.

Conclusion

Although these two views are very clear and separate, many Christians do not fall entirely into one category or the other with their beliefs.

For example, consider the doctrines of the Salvation Army found in the back of their song book. Two of them are as follows:

> "We believe that our first parents were created in a state of innocency, but by their disobedience they lost their purity and happiness, and that in consequence of their fall all men have become sinners, *totally depraved*, and as such are justly exposed to the wrath of God."

> "We believe that continuance in a state of salvation depends upon continued obedient faith in Christ."

As we have seen above, the first of these, the belief in *total depravity,* is basically a Calvinistic doctrine - unless the Salvation Army understands "total depravity" in a different way to Calvinists. However, the second, which implies that a person can lose their salvation if they do not continue in *obedient faith,* is an Arminian doctrine.

Thus there is a mixture of beliefs amongst different groups of Christians and today many Christians are a mixture of both. Possibly the most popular mix is to reject the first four of the main five points of Calvinism, but hold to the fifth.

Although Calvinism tries to uplift God, give Him the glory, and magnify His sovereignty, in the minds of many it casts serious doubt on His goodness and morality, as He chooses some for eternal life but leaves others to suffer the second death, through no fault of their own other than they were not chosen by God.

However, many Christians do not agree that salvation can be lost. On this one point they strongly agree with the Calvinistic doctrine of security of salvation. Many such Christians understand that the passages that refer to loss, as we have seen above, refer to loss of reward in eternal life, rather than loss of the gift of eternal life itself.

―――――――――

If you have found this publication of interest and
help then you may like to read
Salvation: Safe and Secure
by Sylvia Penny.
Details given on the next page.

―――――――――

Salvation: Safe and Secure
By Sylvia Penny

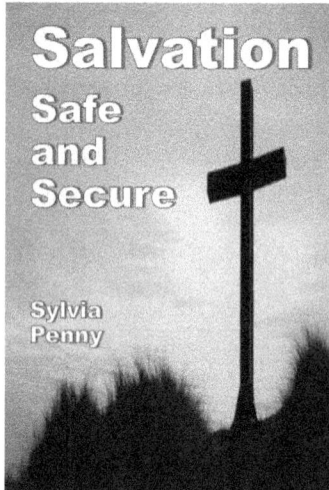

This important book is a thorough treatment of the subject of salvation, asking such questions as …

- What is it, exactly, that saves us?
- Is salvation secure?
- Can it be lost?
- What is 'conditional security'?

It deals with a wide number of issues such as …

- Salvation and works
- The doctrine of rewards

- Lordship salvation
- Free grace theology
- ○ Assurance of salvation
- Why people lose their faith

Further of all this book can be seen on

www.obt.org.uk

It can be ordered from that website and from

The Open Bible trust
Fordland Mount, Upper Basildon,
Reading, RG8 8LU, UK.

It is also available as an eBook
from Amazon and Apple and as a
KDP paperback from Amazon.

About the author

Sylvia Penny was born in Bexleyheath, Kent, in 1956. She was educated at Basingstoke High School and Queen Mary's College, before studying accountancy at Oxford Polytechnic. She qualified as a Chartered Accountant and practised in the profession for a number of years, until she went to live in the USA with her husband and was a pastor's wife, taking an active role in the church. On returning to Britain she went back to the accountancy profession and now works part time as an accountant.

Other publications by Sylvia Penny include the books *Introducing God's Plan* (which she wrote with her husband Michael Penny) and *Salvation: Safe and Secure.* She also collated and edited *Woman to Woman,* a collection of articles for women by women and which has received a number of good reviews. An ideal book for women's ministry.

She has also written a number of booklets including *The Seven Deadly Sins, Loving your Enemies, Lying, Forgiveness, Theories of Creation, Noah's Flood* and *Resurrection: When?* (written with her husband Michael Penny).

Her latest major book is

Satan through the Bible

Details of all these books can be seen on
www.obt.org.uk
They can be ordered from that website and from

The Open Bible trust
Fordland Mount, Upper Basildon,
Reading, RG8 8LU, UK.

They are also available as eBooks
from Amazon and Apple and as
KDP paperbacks from Amazon.

Sylvia Penny is a regular contributor to
Search magazine which is published bi-monthly
by The Open Bible Trust

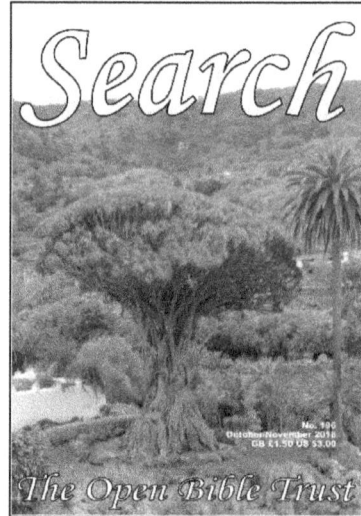

Also by Sylvia Penny

Satan through the Bible

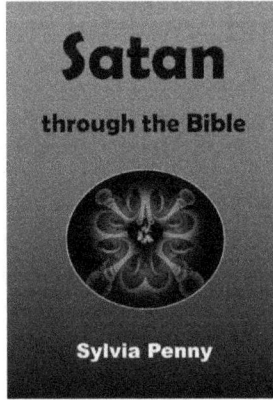

This is a comprehensive treatment of all that the Bible has to say about Satan. Starting with his creation before Eden, it follows him and his activities throughout the Bible, culminating with his demise in the lake of fire.

It considers many of his different names and titles, dealing with what they mean or signify. It discusses such issues as whether or not Satan is omnipresent, and just how much he knows and understands.

And we have details and explanations about every encounter Satan had with people including Eve and Job, Jesus and Judas, Peter and Paul, and many others.

We have a great and powerful enemy, and it is important that we have a Biblical view of who he is, what he is like, and how he can influence both individuals and society today.

****

Further details of this book, and the one on the next page, can be seen on

www.obt.org.uk

They can be ordered from that website and from

The Open Bible trust
Fordland Mount, Upper Basildon,
Reading, RG8 8LU, UK.

They are also available as eBooks
from Amazon and Apple and as
KDP paperbacks from Amazon.

Woman to Woman
By Sylvia Penny

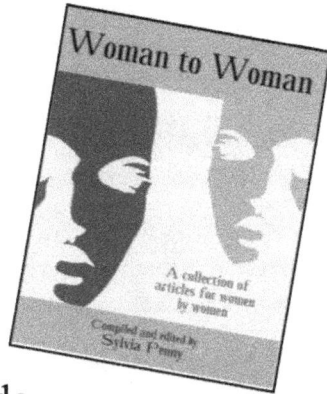

A collection of 60 articles by women for women compiled and edited by Sylvia Penny. Topics include women in the Bible, Greek and Roman women, raising children, teenagers, marriage swearing, abortion, and more.

"This book could be kept to hand for use in precious moments of quiet reflection as time allows – and enjoyed .... The book is nicely presented, about the right price for its size, and would make a very acceptable gift."
(Reviewed by Jan Macgregor in *Evangelicals Now*)

"It is both interesting and helpful .... I enjoyed the book. It is a good resource and easily dipped into."
(Reviewed by Rita Dollar in *Prophecy Today*.)

Arminianism or Calvinism?   69

About this book

Arminianism or Calvinism?

Basically they are two different theological views regarding God's role and our own in the whole process of salvation. Both are based on the Bible, but the differences arise due to their interpretation of what the Bible says.

Calvinism was popularised by John Calvin (1509-1564) who was a French reformer, and followed after Martin Luther (1483-1546) who initiated the Reformation. Arminianism is named after Jacob Arminius (1560-1609) who was a Dutch theologian.

But what are Calvinism and Arminianism? What are the differences? And why does it matter?

Publications of The Open Bible Trust must be in accordance with its evangelical, fundamental and dispensational basis. However, beyond this minimum, writers are free to express whatever beliefs they may have as their own understanding, provided that the aim in so doing is to further the object of The Open Bible Trust. A copy of the doctrinal basis is available on **www.obt.org.uk** or from:

THE OPEN BIBLE TRUST
Fordland Mount, Upper Basildon,
Reading, RG8 8LU, UK.

www.ingramcontent.com/pod-product-compliance
Lightning Source LLC
Chambersburg PA
CBHW020518030426

42337CB00011B/454